Suzanne Torres
Helen Casey

Starlight

C000283187

1 Student Book

Starter Unit
Monty and Lola — 2

Unit 1
Monty the Artist — 6

Unit 2
Lola the Doctor — 18

Game
The Paint Race — 30

Culture
Japan — 31

Unit 3
Monty the Clown — 32

Review Story
Secret Agent 10 — 44

Unit 4
Lola the Pilot — 46

Game
Four in a Row — 58

Culture
India — 59

Unit 5
Monty the Farmer — 60

Unit 6
Lola the Pirate — 72

Game
The Island Game — 84

Culture
Madagascar — 85

Review Story
The History Project — 86

Unit 7
Monty the Magician — 88

Unit 8
Lola the Athlete — 100

Game
Maze Run — 112

Culture
United States of America — 113

Unit 9
Monty the Diver — 114

Review Story
Goal! — 126

OXFORD
UNIVERSITY PRESS

Vocabulary

1 Listen, point and say.

2 Listen and point to the numbers.

3 Listen again and repeat.

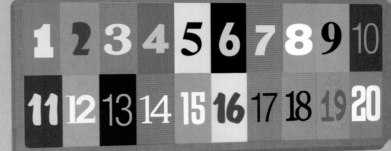

1 2 3 4 5 6 7 8 9 10
11 12 13 14 15 16 17 18 19 20

Hello! I'm Mr. Sonic. What's your name?

I'm Monty.

I'm Lola.

4 Listen, follow and repeat.

One, two, three,
Four, five, six!
How old are you?
How old are you?
Seven, eight, nine,
Ten, eleven, twelve!
How old are you?
How old are you?

Thirteen, fourteen,
Fifteen, sixteen,
Seventeen, eighteen,
Nineteen, twenty!
Hello! Hello!
How old are you?
I'm six! I'm seven! And you?

5 Ask and answer with a friend.

How old are you?

I'm six.

6 **Listen, point and repeat.** 🎧 **04**

7 **Listen and follow. Listen again and say the chant.** 🎧 **05**

One, two, three, four,
Desk, board, window, door.
Trash can, book, teacher, chair,
One girl here, one boy there.

8 **Look and trace the missing letters.**

1 board

2 window

3 door

4 teacher

5 girl

6 boy

7 chair

8 trash can

9 desk

10 book

9 **Play *Number the Objects* with a friend.** 💬

Nine
Yes!

Desk!

3

Our Library

1 Listen and read along. 06

1

Monty and Lola, please bring twenty books!

Yes, Mr. Sonic!

2

Wow! Lots of books!

Space

3

What's that?

It's a door. Let's look!

Space

4

Oh! We're in space! Look! Aliens!

How many aliens are there? One, two, three, four …

5

… five! Oh! Goodbye!

Run!

6

Here are the books, Mr. Sonic.

Oh! Thank you!

2 Act out the story.

1 Count and write the numbers.

1 How many books are there? 6

2 How many chairs are there? ☐

3 How many desks are there? ☐

4 How many boys are there? ☐

2 Look and count. Complete the questions.

boards ~~doors~~ girls teachers

1 How many ____doors____ are there? Four.

2 How many _____ are there? Two.

3 How many _____ are there? One.

4 How many _____ are there? Five.

3 Look around your classroom. Ask and answer with a friend.

How many windows are there?

Yes!

Two!

Please bring the books, Monty!

Our Library

Yes, Mr. Sonic!

1 Monty the Artist

1 Answer with a friend. 💬

  1 How many colors are there?

  2 What colors can you see in your classroom? Point and say.

2 Listen and point. 🎧 07

3 Listen again and repeat.

4 Read and color.

  1 purple

  2 black

  3 green

  4 red

  5 white

  6 blue

  7 brown

  8 pink

  9 yellow

  10 orange

5 Read and circle the colors. Listen and play *Colorful Stand Up*.

I'm an artist.
My painting's big.
It's (red,) green, orange
And yellow and pink.

It's white, black, brown
And purple, too.
But my favorite color
Is blue, blue, blue!

Oh, my favorite color
Is blue, blue, blue!
My favorite color
Is blue!

6 Listen again and sing along.

7 Look and complete the colors.

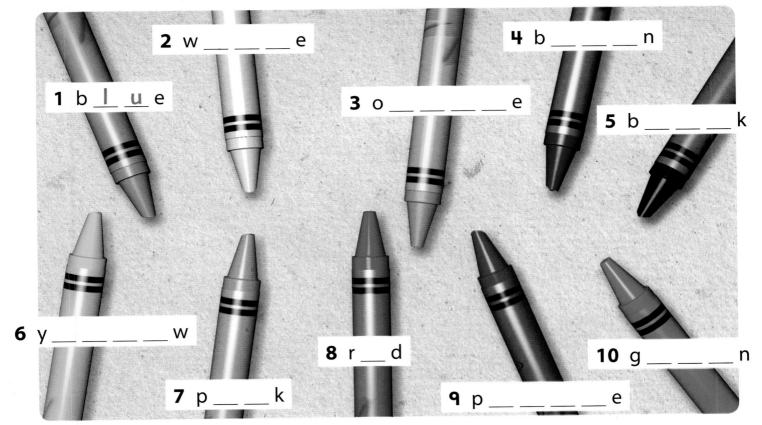

2 w ___ ___ ___ e

4 b ___ ___ ___ n

1 b l u e

3 o ___ ___ ___ ___ ___ e

5 b ___ ___ ___ k

6 y ___ ___ ___ ___ ___ w

8 r ___ d

10 g ___ ___ ___ n

7 p ___ ___ ___ k

9 p ___ ___ ___ ___ ___ e

8 Tell your friend.

My favorite color is orange!

My favorite color is green!

7

The Blue Handprint

1 Look at the pictures and answer with a friend.

1 How many boys and girls are there?   **2** Where's the blue handprint?

2 Listen and read. Mark (✔) the color words in the story. 🎧 09

✔ blue ☐ green ☐ orange ☐ pink ☐ red ☐ yellow

1 Today is art class. The teacher is Mr. Gnome.

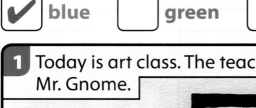

Look at my painting. It's a butterfly.

It's very good.

2 Mr. Gnome sees a handprint on the wall.

Oh no! Look! A handprint!

It's blue.

3 This is Sammy.

This is my paint. *It's red.*

4 This is Daisy.

This is my paint. *It's yellow.*

5 This is Billy.

This is my paint. *It's blue.* My favorite color is blue.

Oh!

6

But my hand is small. This hand is big.

7 Billy has an idea.

Look at your hand, Mr. Gnome!

Oh! *It's blue*!

8 It's Mr. Gnome's handprint.

Oh no! Sorry, children!

It's OK, Mr. Gnome!

3 **Act out the story.** 💬

1 **Listen and number. Look and trace.** 🎧 10

 It's blue.
It's brown.

 It's yellow.
It's green.

 It's pink.
It's purple.

[1]  It's orange.
It's red.

2 **Look and complete the sentences.**

1 It's _____black_____. **3** It's _____. **5** It's _____.

2 _____ red. **4** _____ blue. **6** _____ green.

3 **Look at the picture in Activity 2. Guess with a friend.** 💬

It's red.

The door!

4 Listen and color. 🎧 11

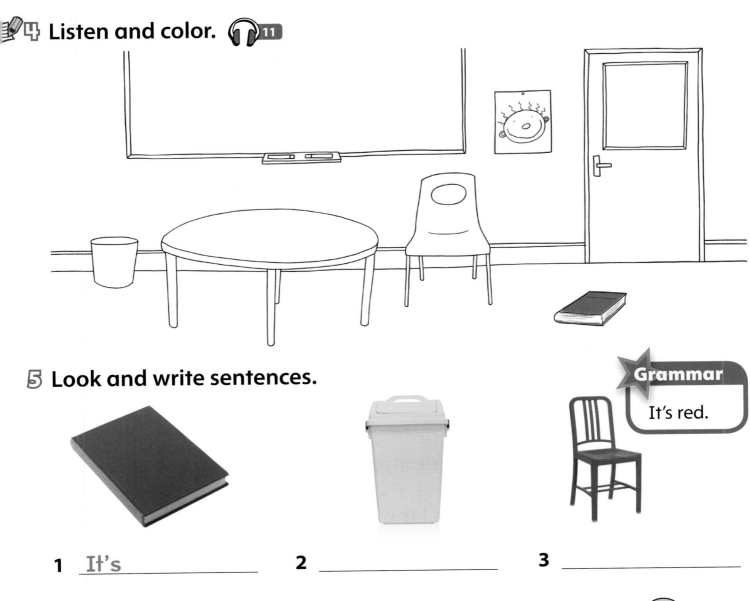

5 Look and write sentences.

Grammar

It's red.

1 It's _____   2 _____   3 _____

6 Use different colors to complete the *Bingo* chart.

7 Play *Bingo* with a friend. 💬

It's green.

It's red.

It's blue.

… Bingo!

Lola's Tune

1 Listen, point and repeat. Trace. 🎧 12

 pencil case

 pencil

 pen

 eraser

 schoolbag

2 Listen and follow. Listen again and sing along. 13

Let's clean up!
Let's clean up!
Let's clean up again!
Let's clean up!
Let's clean up!
Whose is this pen?

It's my pencil.
It's my pen.
It's my pencil case.
Let's clean up again!

Let's clean up!
Let's clean up! …

It's your eraser.
It's your pen.
It's your schoolbag.
Let's clean up again!

Let's clean up!
Let's clean up! …

3 Look at the picture and label the objects.

1 _____ schoolbag _____

2 _____

3 _____

4 _____

5 _____

⁴ Read and circle.

1 It's (my) / your schoolbag.

2 It's my / **your** pencil case.

3 It's my / your eraser.

4 It's my / your pen.

Grammar

It's my book.

It's your pencil case.

⁵ Look and write *my* or *your*.

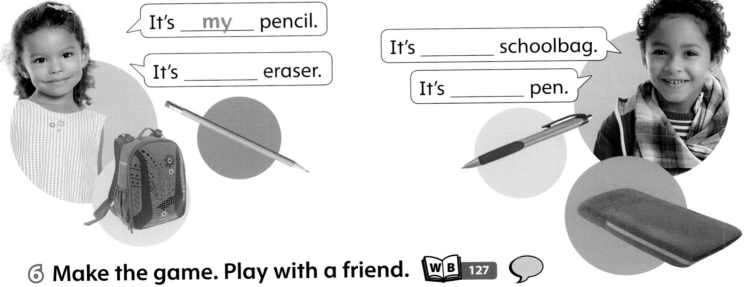

It's ___my___ pencil.

It's _____ eraser.

It's _____ schoolbag.

It's _____ pen.

⑥ Make the game. Play with a friend. 📖ᴮ 127 💬

It's your pencil.
It's blue!

It's my eraser.
It's red!

1 Look at the picture. Count and write.

How many can you see?

1 ● ☐   2 ■ ☐   3 ▬ ☐   4 ▲ ☐

2 Listen and read along. Point to the shapes and colors.

Senecio, Paul Klee

Abstract Art

In *abstract art*, *artists* use different shapes, like ■ *squares*, ▬ *rectangles*, ▲ *triangles* and ● *circles*. They also use many colors.

This *painting* is orange, pink, red, yellow, blue and white.

3 Color and label the shapes.

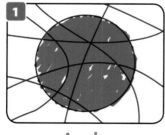 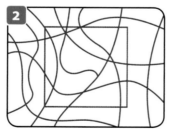 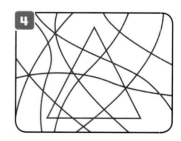

___circle___   _____   _____   _____

4 Look and complete. Listen and check. 🎧 15

| blue   green   circles   squares |

This is my picture. It's _____blue_____, orange and pink. Look! _____!

This is my picture. It's black, _____ and brown. Look! _____ and rectangles!

5 Use shapes to make a picture. Count and write the numbers.

☐ squares

☐ circles

☐ rectangles

☐ triangles

6 Describe your picture. Tell a friend. 💬

This is my picture. It's _____ .

Look! _____ .

1 Trace the letter. Listen and repeat. 🎧 16

artist   big   handprint   pink   six   window

2 Listen and read. 🎧 17

Look! Six handprints! One is blue.
One is pink and yellow, too.
One on the window, one on the wall,
One is big and one is small.

1 2 3 4 5
6 7 8 9 10
11 12 13 14 15
16 17 18 19 20

3 Listen and repeat the chant.

15

A Desk Organizer

Lola's Value ...

Materials

- ★ 1–2 empty paper towel rolls, clean plastic cups and Styrofoam cups
- ★ Scissors
- ★ Glue
- ★ Cardboard
- ★ Colored paints and decorations (glitter, stickers, etc.)
- ★ Paintbrushes

★ **Read and stick.**

Keep your desk organized!

Stage 1: Plan your project.

1 Choose the best material to make your desk organizer.
2 Decide how big your desk organizer needs to be.

Stage 2: Develop your project.

1 Cut the paper towel rolls, plastic cups or Styrofoam cups to different sizes.
2 Glue them on the card.
3 Paint and decorate your desk organizer with colors and shapes.

Stage 3: Share your project.

1 Let's organize! Put your objects in your desk organizer.
2 Show your desk organizer to your classmates.

> Look! It's my desk organizer. It's red, yellow and orange.

Stage 4: Evaluate your project. 14

Save your *Project Record*.

1 **Listen and follow. Say the number.** 🎧 **18**

2 **Look at Activity 1 and write sentences.**

1 It's red. _____

2 ⭐ 6 _____

3 **Color your objects. Color your friend's objects.**

My Objects	My Friend's Objects

4 **Describe the objects.** 💬

This is my eraser. It's yellow.

This is your pencil. It's blue.

17

1 Answer with a friend. 💬

1 Who is the doctor?

2 What colors and objects can you see?

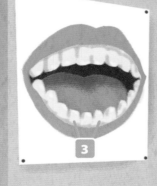

2 Listen and point. 🎧 19

3 Listen again and repeat.

4 Read and trace.

1 face

2 hair

3 teeth

4 nose

5 cheeks

6 mouth

7 eyes

8 ears

9 toes

10 feet

5 Circle ten body words. Write the words.

cheekseyesearsfeetfacehairmouthnoseteethtoes

1 h_____

2 e_____

3 f_____

4 t_____

5 t_____

6 e_____

7 cheeks

8 n_____

9 m_____

10 f_____

6 Circle the body parts. Listen and point to your body. 🎵 20

Doctor! Doctor!
I'm ill today!
Doctor! Doctor!
I'm ill.

Look at my face,
My mouth and my teeth.
Look at my ears.
Look at my feet.

Doctor! Doctor! …

Look at my eyes,
My cheeks and my nose.
Look at my hair.
Look at my toes.

Doctor! Doctor! …

7 Listen again and sing along.

8 Play *Tell the Doctor* with a friend. 💬

Hello. How are you?

I'm ill today. Look at my cheeks.

Poor Mr. Bear!

1 Look at the pictures and answer with a friend.

1 How many bears are there?   **2** Where is Mr. Bear?

2 Listen and read along. Number the speech bubbles in order. 21

Look! I have a mouth.	☐
Here's the doctor.	1
There's Mr. Bear!	☐
Look! I have ears.	☐

5 Then the doctor takes off another bandage.

Look! *I have a nose and eyes.*

Hurray!

6 Then the doctor takes off another bandage.

Look! *I have ears.*

Oh!

That isn't Mr. Bear!

7 It isn't Mr. Bear. It's Mr. Wolf!

Where's Mr. Bear?

Oops!

8 Mr. Bear is in the other bed.

I'm here!

There's Mr. Bear!

Oh no!

3 **Act out the story.**

1 **Listen and number. Match the pictures with the sentences.** 22

1

I have a nose. I have eyes. I have ears. I have a mouth.

2 **Read and circle.**

1 I have **nose** / a nose.

2 I have **toes** / **a toes**.

3 I have **a teeth** / **teeth**.

4 I have **a cheeks** / **cheeks**.

5 I have **mouth** / **a mouth**.

6 I have **feet** / **a feet**.

3 Unscramble the sentences. Look and number the children.

1 have / I / face / a / .

  I have a face.

2 nose / have / . / I / a

_____

3 hair / . / I / have

_____

4 ears / I / . / have

_____

4 Describe the pictures.

1 I have teeth.

2 _____

3 _____

4 _____

5 Play *Body Parts Memory* with your friends. 💬

I have eyes.

I have eyes and a mouth.

I have eyes, a mouth and cheeks.

23

Monty's Tune

1 **Listen, point and repeat.**
Number the words. 🎧 23

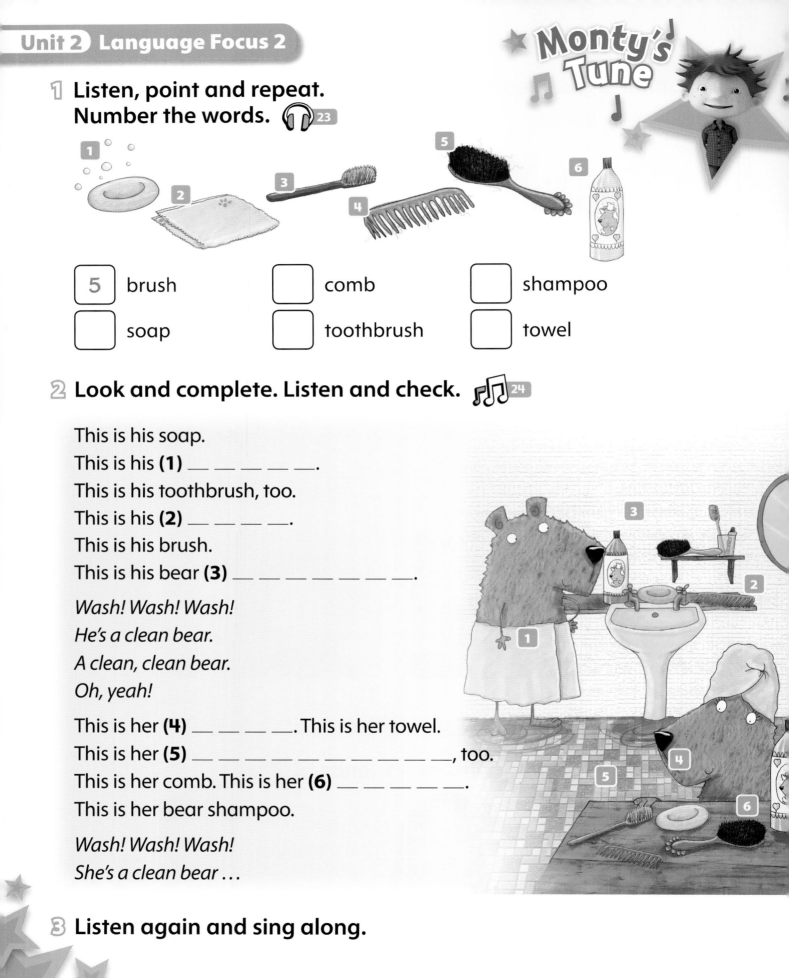

| 5 | brush | | comb | | shampoo |

| | soap | | toothbrush | | towel |

2 **Look and complete. Listen and check.** 🎵 24

This is his soap.
This is his **(1)** __ __ __ __ __.
This is his toothbrush, too.
This is his **(2)** __ __ __ __.
This is his brush.
This is his bear **(3)** __ __ __ __ __ __ __.

Wash! Wash! Wash!
He's a clean bear.
A clean, clean bear.
Oh, yeah!

This is her **(4)** __ __ __ __. This is her towel.
This is her **(5)** __ __ __ __ __ __ __ __ __ __, too.
This is her comb. This is her **(6)** __ __ __ __ __.
This is her bear shampoo.

Wash! Wash! Wash!
She's a clean bear …

3 **Listen again and sing along.**

4 Listen and match. 🎧 25

Grammar

This is his shampoo.
This is her brush.

5 Look and complete with *his* or *her* and the objects.

1 **1** This is ___his towel___.

2 **2** This is _____.

3 **3** This is _____.

4 **4** This is _____.

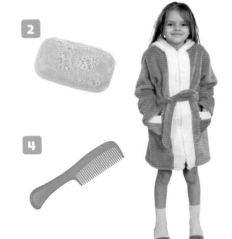

6 Make the game. Play with a friend. 📖 125 💬

This is his soap
and his shampoo.

This is her comb
and her brush.

25

1 **Answer with a friend. How many teeth do you have?**

2 **Listen and read along. Circle the ages.** 26

You get teeth when you are a baby. They are called *baby teeth*.

When you are (three) you have twenty baby teeth.

When you are six, you get *adult teeth*.

When you are fourteen, you have twenty-eight adult teeth.

Take care of your teeth! Use your toothbrush. *Brush your teeth* three times a day!

3 **Read again and count the teeth. Write the ages.**

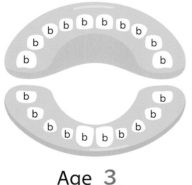

Age <u>3</u>

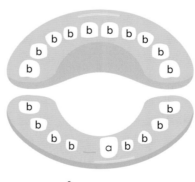

Age ___

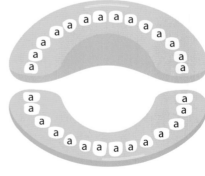

Age ___

4 **Listen and match.** 27

I have twenty baby teeth. I brush my teeth two times a day.

I have sixteen baby teeth. I have two adult teeth. I brush my teeth three times a day.

5 **Count and draw your teeth. Write and circle.**

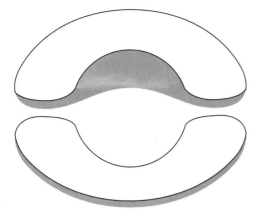

_____ baby **tooth / teeth**
_____ adult **tooth / teeth**

6 **Describe your picture. Tell a friend.**

I have _____ .

I brush _____ .

1 **Listen and circle the _th_ sound.**
Listen again and repeat. 🎧 **28**

ba**th**room   mou**th**   tee**th**   three   thirteen   toothbrush

2 **Listen and read.** 🎧 **29**

Bears in the ba**th**room, one, two, **th**ree.
Mr. Bear, Mrs. Bear, a bear family.
This is baby's too**th**brush. Look at his tee**th**!
Look at his mou**th**! Look at his feet!

3 **Listen again and repeat the chant.**

A Healthy Teeth Poster

Monty's Value ...

Materials

★ Poster paper
★ Pens
★ Magazines
★ Scissors
★ Glue stick

★ **Read and stick.**

Take care of your teeth!

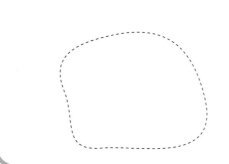

Stage 1: Plan your project.

1 Ask an adult. What is good for your teeth? What is bad for your teeth?

2 Divide your poster into two sections. Draw a tooth on each side. Label the teeth *Good* and *Bad*.

Stage 2: Develop your project.

1 Find pictures in magazines to show what is good and bad for your teeth.

2 Stick your pictures on your poster.

3 Write a title.

Stage 3: Share your project.

Present your poster to your classmates.

> Look! This is soda. It's bad for my teeth.

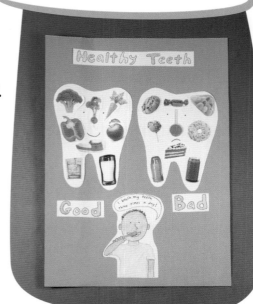

Stage 4: Evaluate your project. 24

Save your *Poster*.

1 Listen, follow and say the number. 🎧 30

2 Look at Activity 1 and write sentences.

1 ⭐1 <u>I have eyes.</u>   2 ⭐7 _____

_____   _____

_____   _____

3 Choose and draw. Write sentences.

brush   ~~comb~~   soap   towel

<u>This is her comb.</u>   _____

_____   _____

1 Play *The Paint Race*.

Start

1 It's ...

2 I have ...

3 This is ...

4 It's my ...

5 It's your ...

6 Go back 2 spaces

7 This is ...

8 It's ...

9 I have ...

10 This is ...

11 It's my ...

12 Go forward 2 spaces

13 It's your ...

14 This is ...

15 It's ...

16 I have ...

17 This is ...

18 Go back 2 spaces

19 It's my ...

20 I have ...

21 This is ...

22 It's ...

Finish!

Japan

1 Answer with a friend. Where do you have lunch?

2 Read the text and number the pictures.

① Hello! I'm Miho. I'm from Japan. I'm in grade 1. I'm six. This is my teacher, Mr. Sato. I help him clean up the classroom!

② Look! I have lunch at school. I eat my lunch in my classroom. Today I have rice, fish and milk. I use *chopsticks*!

③ After lunch, I brush my teeth at school.

chopsticks

3 Read again and complete the chart. Then complete for you.

Name	Age	Teacher	Lunch	Brush Teeth
Miho	6	_____	☐ at school ☐ at home	☐ at school ☐ at home
_____	__	_____	☐ at school ☐ at home	☐ at school ☐ at home

4 Answer with a friend. Is your school the same or different?

Vocabulary

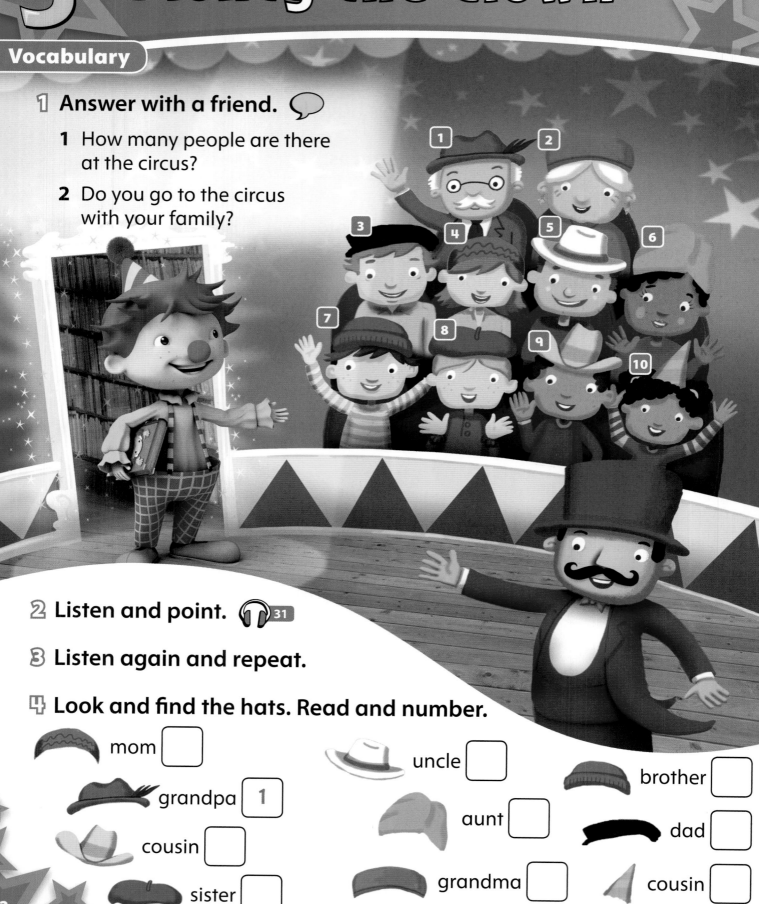

1 Answer with a friend.

1 How many people are there at the circus?

2 Do you go to the circus with your family?

2 Listen and point. 🎧 31

3 Listen again and repeat.

4 Look and find the hats. Read and number.

mom ☐

grandpa 1

cousin ☐

sister ☐

uncle ☐

aunt ☐

grandma ☐

brother ☐

dad ☐

cousin ☐

5 Look and label the family tree.

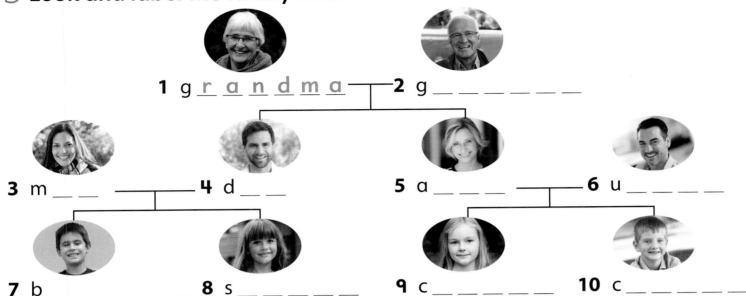

1 g r a n d m a —— 2 g _ _ _ _ _ _ _ _

3 m _ _ _ —— 4 d _ _ _   5 a _ _ _ _ —— 6 u _ _ _ _ _

7 b _ _ _ _ _ _ _   8 s _ _ _ _ _ _   9 c _ _ _ _ _ _ _   10 c _ _ _ _ _ _ _

6 Circle the family pictures in each verse. Listen and sing along. 🎵 32

Come, come, come to the circus,
You and you and you!
Mom and Dad, Brother, Sister,
Come to the circus, too!

Come, come, come to the circus,
You and you and you!
Aunt and Uncle and my cousins,
Come to the circus, too!

Come, come, come to the circus,
You and you and you!
Grandpa, Grandma, yes, you too,
Come to the circus, too!

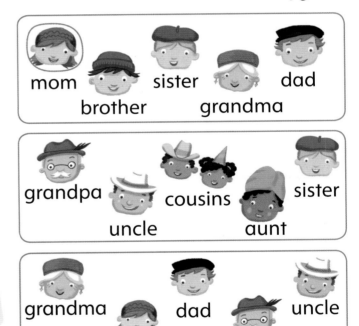

7 Play *Remember the Hats* with a friend. 💬

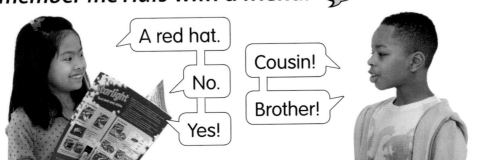

A red hat.

No.

Yes!

Cousin!

Brother!

Jump! Jump! Jump!

1 Look at the pictures and answer with a friend.

1 How many people are there in the family? 2 Who is Bam Bam?

2 Listen and read. Circle the family members in the story. 🎧 33

brother   cousins   dad   grandma   (grandpa)   mom

1 This is Ruby. This is Bam Bam. Bam Bam is in the tree. The tree is very big. Bam Bam is very high up.

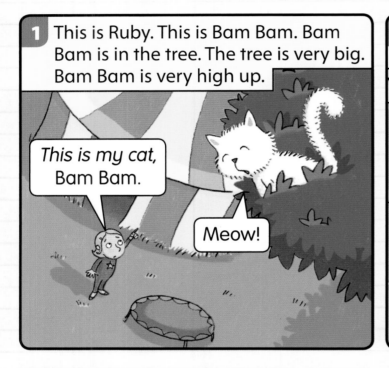

This is my cat, Bam Bam.

Meow!

2 This is Grandpa. Grandpa jumps, but Bam Bam is very high up.

This is my grandpa.

Oh no!

3 This is Dad. Dad jumps. He jumps onto Grandpa, but Bam Bam is very high up.

This is my dad.

Oh no!

4 These are Ruby's cousins. The cousins jump. They jump onto Dad, but Bam Bam is very high up.

These are my cousins.

Oh no!

5 This is Grandma. Grandma jumps. She jumps onto Ruby's cousins, but Bam Bam is very high up.

This is my grandma.

Oh no!

6 Grandma, the cousins, Dad and Grandpa have an idea.

Jump, Ruby!

Me?

7 Jump, jump, jump!

Hello, Bam Bam!

Meow!

8 Here's Bam Bam the cat. Now Bam Bam is happy.

Thank you, everyone!

3 Act out the story. 💬

35

1 **Read and number. Listen, point and say the number.**

1 This is my dad.

2 This is my grandpa.

3 These are my cousins.

4 This is my grandma.

2 **Look, read and circle.**

This is my family.

1 (This is) / **These are** my grandma.

2 **This is** / **These are** my sisters.

3 **This is** / **These are** my mom.

4 **This is** / **These are** my uncles.

3 **Look and write *This is* or *These are*.**

1 <u> This is </u> my mom.

2 _____ my grandpa.

3 _____ my uncle.

4 _____ my sisters.

5 _____ my brothers.

4 **Draw your family. Play *The Family Game* with a friend.**

These are my cousins.

No.

Yes!

Number 2 and number 3!

Number 4 and number 5!

Lola's Tune

1 **Listen, point and repeat. Match.** 35

long hair   blond hair   small eyes

gray hair   big eyes   short hair

2 **Circle the descriptions. Listen and sing along.** 36

It's Grandpa! Grandpa!
Look over there!
He has blue eyes. He has gray hair.
It's Grandpa! Grandpa!
Look over there!
He has small eyes. He has short hair.

Jump, jump, Grandpa!
Jump, Grandpa, jump!
Jump, jump, Grandpa!
Jump, Grandpa, jump!

It's Grandma! Grandma!
Look over there!
She has green eyes. She has blond hair.
It's Grandma! Grandma!
Look over there!
She has big eyes. She has long hair.

Jump, jump, Grandma!
Jump, Grandma, jump!
Jump, jump, Grandma!
Jump, Grandma, jump!

3 **Look and complete.**

| big eyes | blond hair | blue eyes | green eyes |
| gray hair | long hair | short hair | small eyes |

Grandpa has ...	Grandma has ...

4 Look and read. Write *yes* or *no*.

1 The girl has long hair.   no

2 Grandma has blond hair. _____

3 Dad has small eyes. _____

4 Mom has big eyes. _____

5 The boy has blue eyes. _____

6 Grandpa has gray hair. _____

> **Grammar**
>
> She has blond hair.
>
> He has green eyes.

5 Complete the sentences about the people in Activity 4.

1 Grandpa has __big eyes_____. He has _____.

2 Dad _____. He _____.

3 Mom _____

6 Write the names of two people in your family. Write descriptions.

____Mom____ _____

_____ _____

7 Make the game. Play with a friend. WB 123

He has big eyes.

He has short hair.

1 Describe someone in your family to a friend. 💬

2 Listen and read along. Label the picture. 🎧 37

Alice   Dad   Lily and Anna   ~~Mom~~

Twins

I'm Alice. This is my family.

My mom has brown eyes. My dad has blue eyes. They're *different*.

I have brown hair and brown eyes. I look like my mom. We're *similar*!

I have two sisters. Lily has blond hair. Can you see Lily?

Anna has blond hair, too! They're *identical*! They're *twins*!

Mom

3 Look and circle the best words.

similar / different   similar / identical   similar / identical   similar / different

4 Listen and write *M* (Monty) or *L* (Lola). 🎧 38

This is my cousin. He has blue eyes. I have brown eyes. We're different.

This is my sister. She has brown hair. I have brown hair. We're similar.

5 Draw and color yourself and a family member.

6 Describe your picture. Tell a friend. 💬

This is me and my _____. My _____.

I have _____.

1 Listen and write the missing sound. Listen again and repeat. 🎧 39

broth**er**   eras**er**   flow**er**   sist**er**   spid**er**   teach____

2 Listen and read. 🎧 40

This is my broth**er**, my sist**er** and me.
This is my teach**er** and her family.
The clown has a flow**er**. It's yellow and blue.
He has a balloon and a spid**er**, too!

3 Listen again and repeat the chant.

A Family Tree

Lola's Value...

Materials

★ Poster paper
★ Brown paint
★ Green and yellow colored paper
★ Scissors
★ Glue stick

★ **Read and stick.**

Spend time with your family.

Stage 1: Plan your project.

1 Write the names of the people in your family.

2 Count the words. How many people are in your family?

Stage 2: Develop your project.

1 Draw a tree on poster paper. Paint it brown.

2 Cut out a leaf for each person in your family.

3 Draw and label a family member on each leaf.

4 Group the pictures. Which people are from your mom's family? Which people are from your dad's family?

5 Stick your leaves onto your tree. Think about how you can show the family links.

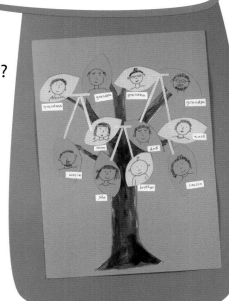

Stage 3: Share your project.

Present your Family Tree to a friend.

Look! This is my family tree. This is my grandma. This is my dad.

Stage 4: Evaluate your project. W B 36

Save your *Family Tree*.

1 Listen, follow and say the number. 41

2 Look at Activity 1 and write sentences.

1 **3** _This is my uncle._

2 **8** _____

_____

_____

3 Draw and describe someone in your class.

This is my friend.

_____

_____

_____

_____

_____

_____

_____

Secret Agent 10

1 **Look at the pictures and answer with a friend.** 💬

1 Where are Monty and Lola? **2** Who are the secret agents?

2 **Listen and read along. Circle the words. Which ones does Secret Agent 10 have?** 🎧 42

blond hair   (brown eyes)   blue eyes   a black hat   big feet   a white hat

1 Monty and Lola are in the classroom at school.

I'm your teacher today. Mr. Sonic isn't here.

Please bring the books, Monty and Lola!

OK! Come on, Lola!

2 Now Monty and Lola are in a city.

I'm secret Agent 8. You're Secret Agent 9.

I have a bag and a book. Look!

3 Lola opens the book. Monty and Lola read.

Top Secret

Find Secret Agent 10!
He has black hair.
He has brown eyes.
He has a white hat.
He has big feet.

4 Monty and Lola see a white hat.

Look! It's Secret Agent 10!

No! He has brown hair and blue eyes.

5 Then Monty and Lola see big feet.

Look! It's Secret Agent 10!

No, it's a girl. She has blond hair and green eyes.

6 Then Monty and Lola see a door.

What's this?

It's a secret message.

Top Secret

7 Lola has an idea. She opens her bag.

I have a special pen.

Top Secret

Hello, Monty and Lola! From Secret Agent 10.

8 Suddenly, the door opens!

Secret Agent 10!

Mr. Sonic is Secret Agent 10!

Surprise! Come on! Let's go back to our library!

3 Act out the story. 💬

4 Lola the Pilot

Vocabulary

1 Answer with a friend. 💬

1 What color are the clothes?
2 Who do you go on vacation with?

2 Listen, point and repeat. 🎧 43

3 Read and match.

| **1** hat | **2** sweater | **3** T-shirt | **4** jacket | **5** shirt |
| **6** dress | **7** skirt | **8** pants | **9** socks | **10** shoes |

4 Solve the crossword puzzle.

Across →

Down ↓

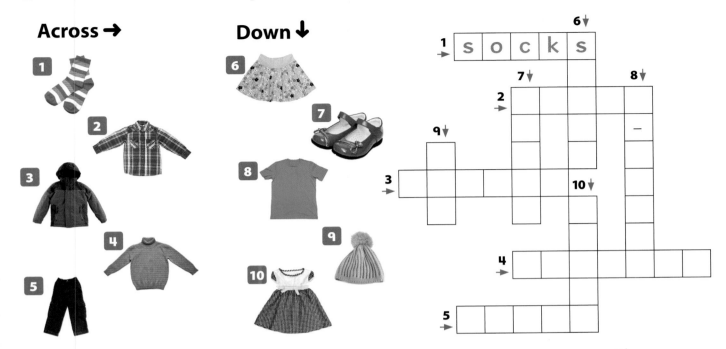

5 Circle your clothes. Listen and play *Fashion Stand Up!* 🎵 44

Let's fly! Let's fly! Let's fly away!
Let's fly! Let's fly away today!

Pack your (shoes.) Let's fly!
Pack your socks. Let's fly!
Pack your pants. Let's fly tonight!
Pack your hat. Let's fly!
Pack your shirt. Let's fly!
Pack your jacket. Let's fly!
That's right!

Let's fly! Let's fly! Let's fly away! …

Pack your shoes. Let's fly!
Pack your socks. Let's fly!
Pack your sweater. Let's fly tonight!
Pack your dress. Let's fly!
Pack your skirt. Let's fly!
Pack your T-shirt. Let's fly!
That's right!

Let's fly! Let's fly! Let's fly away! …

6 Listen again and sing along.

7 Play *Clothes Memory* with your friends. 💬

Pack your socks.

Pack your socks and hat.

Pack your socks, hat and pants.

On Vacation

1 **Look at the pictures and answer with a friend.**

  1 What clothes do they pack?   **2** Are the vacations similar or different?

2 **Listen and read along. Circle Pippa's clothes red. Circle Mickey's clothes blue.** 🎧 45

hat   jacket   shoes   socks   (sweater)   T-shirt

1 This is Pippa the polar bear. She has her suitcase.

I have my sweater and my socks.

I have my jacket.

2 This is Mickey the monkey. He has his suitcase, too.

I have my T-shirt and my hat. I have my shoes.

3 Pippa is at the airport. Mickey is at the airport, too.

Hello, Mickey! How are you?

I'm fine, thank you.

It's time to go.

Bye-bye, Pippa!

Bye-bye, Mickey!

4 Now Pippa is on vacation. She's in the Arctic. It's very cold.

Oh no! A T-shirt, a hat and shoes!

5 Now Mickey is on vacation, too. He's in the jungle. It's very hot.

Oh no! A sweater, a jacket and socks!

6 Poor Pippa!

Hello, Mickey. I'm in the Arctic. It's very cold. *I'm wearing shoes, a T-shirt and a hat!* Brr!

7 Poor Mickey!

Hello, Pippa. I'm in the jungle. It's very hot. *I'm wearing a sweater and socks!* Phew!

8 Mickey sends Pippa's suitcase. Pippa sends Mickey's suitcase.

Hurray!

Hurray!

URGENT! SEND TO PIPPA

URGENT! SEND TO MICKEY

Now Pippa and Mickey are happy.

3 Act out the story.

1 **Listen and circle *Yes* or *No*.** 46

1 (Yes)/ No   **2** Yes / No   **3** Yes / No   **4** Yes / No

2 **Read and write the names.**

| Kim | Sam | Anna | Lucy | Tom | Grace |

1 I'm wearing a skirt and a T-shirt. I'm wearing a sweater.   Grace

2 I'm wearing a sweater and pants. I'm wearing a hat.   _____

3 I'm wearing socks and a skirt. I'm wearing a jacket.   _____

4 I'm wearing pants and a shirt. I'm wearing shoes.   _____

3 **Look at the pictures in Activity 2 and complete the sentences.**

Anna: I'm wearing _____ a skirt _____ and _____.

I'm _____.

Lucy: I'm _____ and _____.

_____.

4 Listen and mark (✔). 🎧 47

1 Who is Nick?

a ✔   **b** ☐   **c** ☐

2 What is Lucy wearing?

a ☐   **b** ☐   **c** ☐

3 Which is Anna?

a ☐   **b** ☐   **c** ☐

4 What is Tom wearing?

a ☐   **b** ☐   **c** ☐

5 Play *Mime and Guess* with a friend. 💬

I'm wearing …

… a T-shirt!

No!

… a hat!

Yes!

★ **Monty's Tune**

1 **Listen, point and repeat.**
  Number the phrases. 🎧 48

| 1 | 2 | 3 | 4 | 5 | 6 |

☐ It's snowing.　　☐ It's cold.　　☐ It's sunny.

☐ It's windy.　　☐ It's raining.　　☐ It's hot.

2 **Circle the weather words. Listen and sing along.** 🎵 49

It's (snowing.) It's snowing.
It's windy and it's cold
In the Arctic! In the Arctic!
It's snowing. It's snowing.
It's windy and it's cold
On my Arctic holiday!

It's raining. It's raining.
It's sunny and it's hot
In the jungle! In the jungle!
It's raining. It's raining.
It's sunny and it's hot
On my jungle holiday!

It's snowing. It's snowing. …

It's raining. It's raining. …

3 **Look and tell a friend. What's the weather like?** 💬

What's the weather like?

It's sunny.

4 Look and complete the weather report. Act it out with a friend.

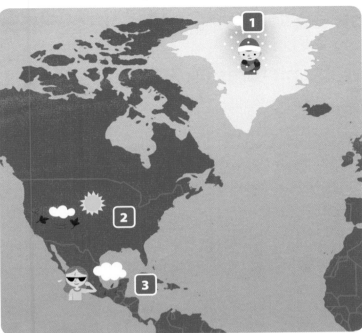

1 Today in the Arctic

it's snowing

and _____.

2 Today in the US

_____

and _____.

3 Today in Mexico

_____

_____.

5 Draw the weather today. Write sentences.

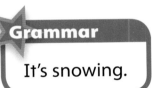
Grammar

It's snowing.

Today in _____

_____

_____

_____

6 Make the game. Play with a friend.

It's snowing in the Arctic.

It's sunny in the jungle.

1 **Answer with a friend.**

1 What's the weather like in the Arctic?   **2** What's the weather like in the jungle?

2 **Listen and read along. Number the pictures.** 50

Climate is the normal weather in a place. Different places around the world have different climates. Different animals and plants live in different climates.

Climates

1 The jungle is hot and rainy. The jungle has big *trees*. *Monkeys* live in the jungle.

2 The *desert* is hot and sunny. The desert has *cactuses*. *Lizards* live in the desert.

3 The Arctic is cold and it's windy. The Arctic has *snow*. *Polar bears* live in the Arctic.

3 **Read and circle the odd one out. Write the climate.**

1 snowy   polar bear   (cactus)   cold   _____the Arctic_____

2 hot   big trees   cactus   lizard   _____

3 hot   rainy   monkey   snowy   _____

4 **Listen and circle.** 51

I'm in the **desert** / (jungle). It's **hot** / **cold**.

I'm in the **jungle** / **Arctic**. It's **hot** / **cold**.

5 Choose a climate. Draw yourself in the climate.

6 Describe your picture. Tell a friend. 💬

I'm _____.

It's _____.

1 Trace the letter and complete the words.
Listen and repeat. 🎧 52

U

br _u_ sh    f __ n    j __ mp    j __ ngle   s __ nny    __ ncle

2 Listen and read. 🎧 53

In the jungle, I jump and swing,
It's sunny and it's hot.
I'm in the jungle with Mom and Uncle.
It's sunny and it's fun.

3 Listen again and repeat the chant.

A Weather Station

Monty's Value ...

Materials

- ★ A plastic bottle with the top cut off
- ★ Small stones
- ★ Water
- ★ A marker pen
- ★ A ruler
- ★ Glue

★ **Read and stick.**

Work together.

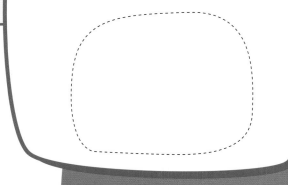

 Stage 1: Plan your project.

1 What can you measure with the Weather Station?

2 Draw a chart in your notebook. Draw two spaces for each day.

Stage 2: Develop your project.

1 Put the stones in your plastic bottle. Add water.

2 Mark a line on the bottle where the water level is.

3 From the water level, mark each centimeter (cm).

4 Glue the top of the plastic bottle on.

5 Take turns visiting your weather station every day. Draw the day's weather on your chart. Write the rain level.

Stage 3: Share your project.

Compare your results with another group.

Stage 4: Evaluate your project. 48

Save your *Weather Station chart*.

Day 1. It's raining.
The rain level is 1 cm.

1 Listen, follow and color the number. 🎧54

2 Look at Activity 1 and write sentences.

1 ⭐6 I'm wearing socks.

2 ⭐2 _____

3 Write sentences.

1 It's windy.

2 _____

3 _____

4 _____

1 Play *Four in a Row*.

This is ...

She has ...

I'm wearing ...

It's ...

He has ...

I'm wearing ...

It's ...

These are ...

I'm wearing ...

It's ...

This is ...

She has ...

It's ...

This is ...

He has ...

I'm wearing ...

India

1 Answer with a friend. Do you have special clothes for festivals? 💬

2 Read the text and label the clothes.

dress ~~sari~~ sherwani

____dress____

Hello! I'm Pia. I'm from India. This is my family. Today is a special day. It's *Diwali*. Diwali is an Indian festival. We wear special clothes. I'm wearing a new dress.

Look at my aunt and my grandma! This Indian dress is called a *sari*. My aunt has a red sari. My uncles and my cousin have long jackets called *sherwanis*.

_____

_____

3 Draw and label the clothes. What do people wear for special days?

Special Clothes in India	Special Clothes in My Country
Special Day: _____	Special Day(s): _____

5 Monty the Farmer

1 Answer with a friend. 💬

  1 How many animals are there?

  2 What's your favorite animal?

2 Listen, point and repeat. 🎧 55

3 Read and trace.

1 bird		**6**	rabbit
2 bull		**7**	chicken
3 horse		**8**	sheep
4 cow		**9**	frog
5 goat		**10**	duck

4 Listen and say the animal. 🎧 56

5 **Look and label the animals.**

1 chick _e_ _n_   **2** sh __ __ __   **3** ho __ __ __   **4** b __ __ __ __   **5** g __ __ __

6 b __ __ __   **7** rabb __ __   **8** __ __ __ __ __   **9** __ __ __ __ __   **10** __ __ __ __

6 **Circle the animals. Listen and say the animal sounds.** 🎵 **57**

Here's a horse.
Here's a sheep.
Here's a bird.
Tweet, tweet, tweet!
Here's a bull.
Here's a goat.
Here's a frog,
Croak, croak, croak!

Chicken, duck,
Rabbit, cow.
Here they are
Down on the farm.
Chicken, duck,
Rabbit, cow.
They're all on the farm.

Here's a horse …

7 **Listen again and sing along.**

8 **Play** *Farmyard Noises* **with a friend.** 💬

Mooo!

No.

Yes!

A bull!

A cow!

Ugly Bird

1 Look at the pictures and answer with a friend.

1 What animals can you see?

2 What color is the ugly bird?

2 Listen and read along. Number the speech bubbles in order. 58

It isn't a frog! ☐

It isn't a chicken! 1

It's a swan! ☐

It isn't a cow! ☐

1 An ugly bird is on a farm. The ugly bird sees a chicken.

Where's my mom?

Are you my mom?

No! I'm not your mom.

2 The chickens laugh.

It isn't a chicken!

It isn't brown and red!

It's gray and ugly!

3 Then the ugly bird sees a cow.

Are you my mom?

No! I'm not your mom.

4 The cows laugh.

It isn't a cow!

It's gray and ugly!

It isn't black and white!

5 Then the ugly bird sees a frog.

6 Suddenly the animals see a big, white bird.

7 The ugly bird sees the swan.

8 Now the ugly bird is with his mom.

3 Act out the story. 💬

63

1 Look and read. Mark (✔) or (✗).

1  It's a horse. ✗

2 It's a frog. ☐

3  It's a bull. ☐

4 It's a swan. ☐

2 Listen and circle the animal. 🎧 59

1

2

3

4

3 Look at the pictures in Activity 2 and number the sentences.

It isn't a duck. It's a rabbit. [2]

It isn't a bull. It's a goat. ☐

It isn't a horse. It's a bird. ☐

It isn't a cow. It's a sheep. ☐

4 Find and color the animals. Write sentences.

1 (rabbit) <u>It isn't a rabbit.</u> <u>It's a frog.</u>

2 (bull) _____ _____

3 (duck) _____ _____

4 (frog) _____ _____

5 (goat) _____ _____

5 Choose three animals. Play *Guess the Animal* with a friend.

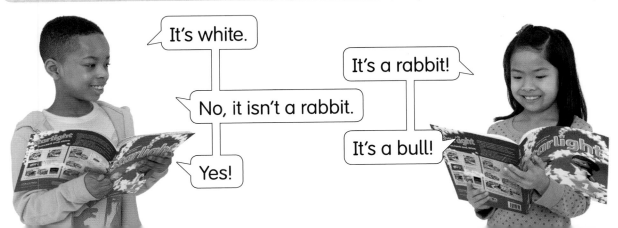

It's white.

No, it isn't a rabbit.

Yes!

It's a rabbit!

It's a bull!

65

Lola's Tune

1 **Listen, point and repeat. Trace.** 🎧 60

calf   chick   foal   kid   lamb

2 **Listen and point to the animals. Listen again and sing along.** 🎵 61

Oh dear! Where's my chick?
Where's my chick? Quick, quick, quick!
Oh dear! Where's my chick?
Where's my chick? Quick, quick!

Here's a calf and here's a kid.
The calf and kid are here.
Here's a calf and here's a kid.
But where's my chick? Oh dear!

Oh dear! Where's my chick? …

Here's a lamb and here's a foal.
The lamb and foal are here.
Here's a lamb and here's a foal.
But where's my chick? Oh dear!

It's here! Here's my chick!
Here's my chick! Chick, chick, chick!
It's here! Here's my chick!
Here's my chick! It's here!

3 **Look at the picture in Activity 2 and number the animals.**

Where's the chick? It's here.   `5`

Where's the foal? It's here.   ☐

Where's the kid? It's here.   ☐

Where's the lamb? It's here.   ☐

Where's the calf? It's here.   ☐

4 Solve and find. Answer the questions.

1 Where's my calf?

2 Where's my kid?

3 Where's my foal?

4 Where's my lamb?

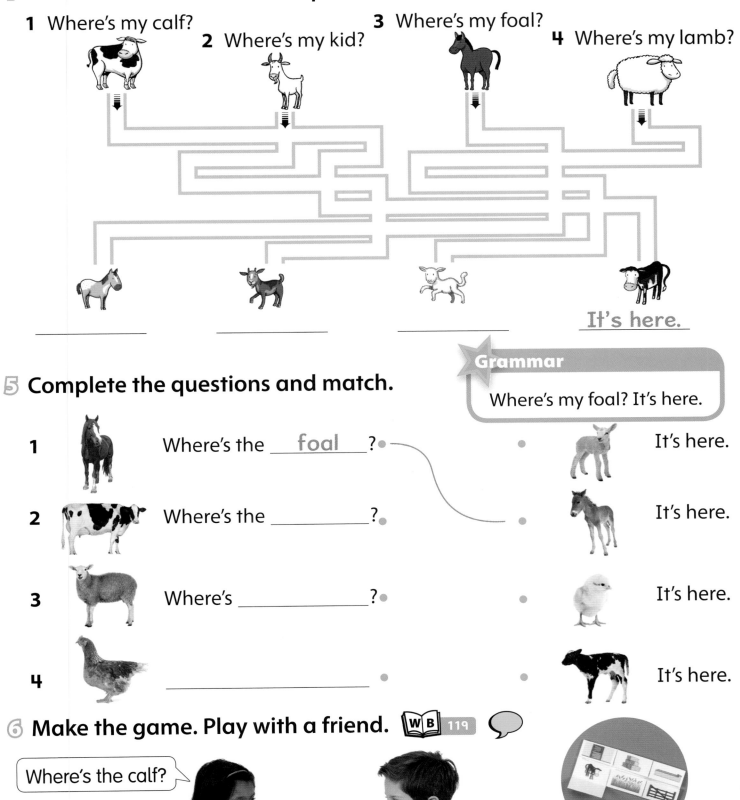

_____   _____   _____   It's here.

5 Complete the questions and match.

Grammar

Where's my foal? It's here.

1 Where's the ___foal___?●

●   It's here.

2 Where's the _____?●

●   It's here.

3 Where's _____?●

●   It's here.

4 _____●

●   It's here.

6 Make the game. Play with a friend. WB 119

Where's the calf?

It's here.

1 **Answer with a friend. What's your favorite music?** 💬

2 **Listen and read along. Point to the animals and instruments.** 🎧 62

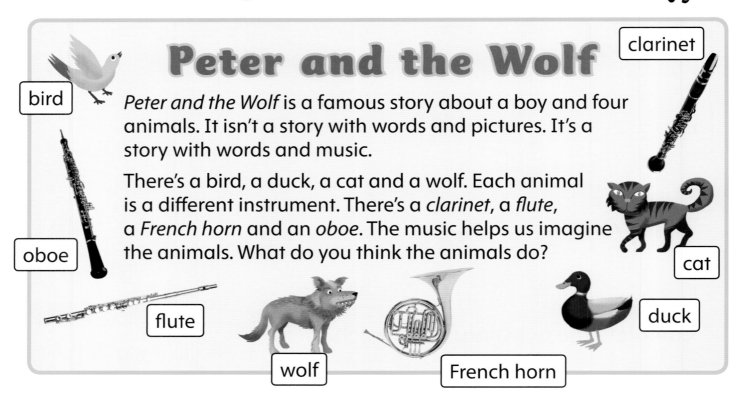

clarinet

bird

Peter and the Wolf

Peter and the Wolf is a famous story about a boy and four animals. It isn't a story with words and pictures. It's a story with words and music.

There's a bird, a duck, a cat and a wolf. Each animal is a different instrument. There's a *clarinet*, a *flute*, a *French horn* and an *oboe*. The music helps us imagine the animals. What do you think the animals do?

oboe

cat

flute

duck

wolf

French horn

3 **Listen and imagine the animals. Listen again and match.** 🎧 63

1 French horn   **2** oboe   **3** flute   **4** clarinet

bird   wolf   cat   duck

4 **Listen and check your ideas.** 🎧 64

5 **Look and complete. Listen and check.** 🎧 65

This is a f <u>l</u> <u>u</u> <u>t</u> <u>e</u>. It's the b __ __ __.

This is a c __ __ __ __ __ __ __ __ __.
It's the c __ __.

6 **Draw an animal and its instrument.**

7 **Describe your drawing. Tell a friend.** 💬

This is _____ . It's _____ .

1 **Listen and circle the sound. Listen and repeat.** 🎧 66

chair   cheeks   chick   chicken   chocolates   teacher

2 **Listen and read.** 🎧 67

Here's a **ch**ick and a **ch**icken, too.
Here are **ch**ocolates for me and you.
Here's a tea**ch**er. She's on a **ch**air.
She has pink **ch**eeks and long, black hair.

3 **Listen again and repeat the chant.**

Cardboard Kazoo

 Lola's Value ...

Materials

★ Different sized cardboard tubes

★ Paint and decorations

★ A square of wax paper

★ A rubber band

★ **Read and stick.**

Listen to your friends.

Stage 1: Plan your project.

1 Look at the picture. Do you think the kazoos make the same sound?

2 Decide how big to make your kazoo. Choose your cardboard tube.

Stage 2: Develop your project.

1 Paint and decorate your cardboard tube.

2 Make a hole in the top of your kazoo.

3 Play your instrument. Does it make a sound?

4 Attach a square of wax paper to one end of your kazoo. Use a rubber band.

5 Play your instrument again. Does it make a different sound?

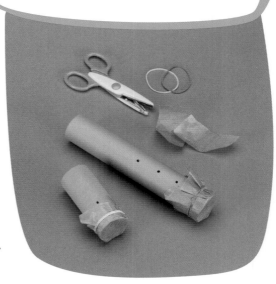

Stage 3: Share your project.

1 Work in small groups. Practice playing your instruments together.

2 Play your instruments for the rest of the class.

This is my kazoo! Listen. It's a duck!

Stage 4: Evaluate your project. 60

Save your *Project Record*.

1 **Listen, follow and color the number.** 68

1 ⭐ 1 ⭐ 2 ⭐ 3 ⭐ 4 ⭐ 5 ⭐ 6 ⭐ 7 ⭐ 8

2 **Look at Activity 1 and write sentences.**

1 ⭐3 <u>It isn't a goat.</u>   <u>It's a duck.</u>

_____   _____

_____   _____

3 **Write questions. Ask and answer with a friend.**

1 <u>Where's the kid?</u>

2 _____

3 _____

Where's the kid?

It's here!

71

6 Lola the Pirate

Vocabulary

1 Answer with a friend.

1 What colors can you see?

2 What's your favorite fruit?

2 Listen, point and repeat. 🎧 69

3 Read and match.

apple	banana	coconut	grape	lemon
lime	mango	orange	pear	pineapple

Unscramble the letters to write the words.

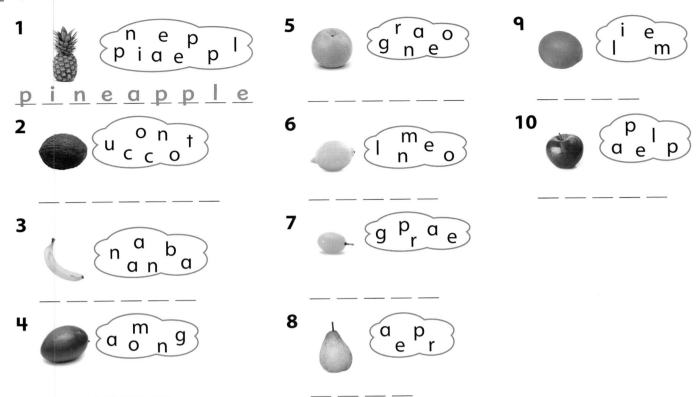

1. p i n e a p p l e

2. _ _ _ _ _ _ _

3. _ _ _ _ _ _

4. _ _ _ _ _

5. _ _ _ _ _ _

6. _ _ _ _ _

7. _ _ _ _ _

8. _ _ _ _

9. _ _ _ _

10. _ _ _ _ _

5 Listen and point to the pictures. Listen again and sing along. 🎵 70

A mango! A mango!
An orange, a pear and a coconut, too.
A grape, a banana and a lemon, too.
An apple, a lime and a pineapple, too.

I'm a pirate on a pirate ship.
I'm a pirate on a pirate ship.
I'm a pirate on a pirate ship.
I'm a pirate on a pirate ship.

A mango! A mango! …

6 Play *Shopping Basket* with a friend. 💬

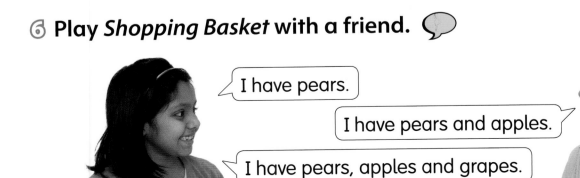

I have pears.

I have pears and apples.

I have pears, apples and grapes.

Fruit Salad

1 **Look at the pictures and answer with a friend.**

1 Who are the people in the story?   **2** What's the weather like?

2 **Listen and read along. Mark (✔) the fruit in the story.**

☐ apples   ☐ bananas   ☐ coconuts   ✔ mangoes   ☐ pineapples

1 Here's a pirate ship. Here are the pirates. Pirate Pete sees mangoes.

Let's pick the mangoes! Who can help?

Not me!

Not me!

Not me! *I don't like monkeys.*

2 So Pirate Pete picks the mangoes.

Phew! It's hot!

But *I like mangoes.*

3 Then Pirate Pete sees pineapples.

Let's pick the pineapples! Who can help?

Not me!

Not me!

Not me! *I don't like frogs.*

4 So Pirate Pete picks the pineapples.

Phew! It's hot!

But *I like pineapples.*

5 Then Pirate Pete sees bananas.

Let's pick the bananas! Who can help?

Not me!

Not me!

Not me! *I don't like big trees.*

6 So Pirate Pete picks the bananas.

Phew! It's hot!

But *I like bananas.*

7 Now Pirate Pete has a fruit salad.

My fruit salad is ready to eat! Who can help?

Oh! Me, please!

Me please!

Me, too! I'm hungry!

8 But Pirate Pete eats the fruit salad.

Sorry, pirates! It's my fruit salad!

Aww!

3 Act out the story. 💬

1 Listen and mark (✔) or (✗). 🎧 72

2 Look and circle *like* or *don't like*.

1 I (like) / don't like bananas.

2 I like / don't like monkeys.

3 I like / don't like frogs.

4 I like / don't like fruit salad.

5 I like / don't like pineapples.

3 Look at the chart and complete the sentences.

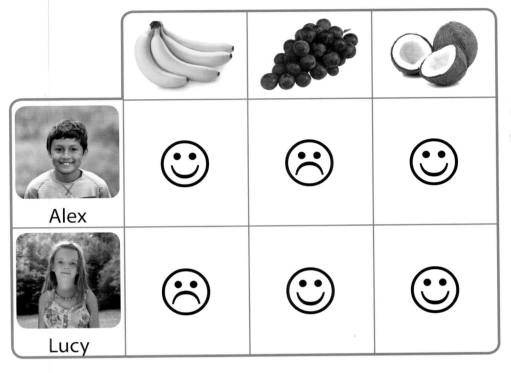

Grammar

I like pears.

I don't like limes.

Alex: <u>I like</u> bananas. _____ grapes. _____ coconuts.

Lucy: _____ bananas. _____ grapes. _____ coconuts.

4 Mark (✔) or (✗) the fruit you like and don't like. Write sentences.

✔ <u>I like oranges.</u>

5 Compare answers with a friend. 💬

I like oranges.

I don't like oranges.
I like apples.

Monty's Tune

1 Listen, point and repeat. Match. 🎧 73

Jell-O   lemonade   fruit salad

smoothie   yogurt   juice

2 Listen and point to the food. Listen again and sing along. 🎵 74

Do you like smoothies?
Do you like smoothies?
Yes, I do!
I like smoothies.
I do! I do!
I do! I do!
I do! I do!

Fruit salad, Jell-O!
Fruit salad, Jell-O!
I like juice. I like Jell-O,
Lemonade, too.
I do! I do!
I do! I do!

Do you like yogurt?
Do you like yogurt?
No, I don't!
I don't like yogurt.
I don't! I don't!
I don't! I don't!
Fruit salad, Jell-O! …

3 Look and complete the questions.

Do you like **(1)** <u>smoothies</u>?

Do you like **(2)** _____?

Do you like **(3)** _____?

Do you like **(4)** _____?

Do you like **(5)** _____?

Do you like **(6)** _____?

4 Read and match.

Do you like smoothies? ☺

> Yes, I do.

Do you like lemonade? ☹

> No, I don't.

Do you like fruit salad? ☺

Do you like Jell-O? ☹

Do you like yogurt? ☺

Do you like juice? ☹

5 Write questions and answer for you. Ask a friend and mark (✔) or (✘). 💬

		Me	My friend
	Do you like juice?	_____	☐
	_____	_____	☐
	_____	_____	☐
	_____	_____	☐

6 Make the game. Play with a friend. WB 117 💬

Say a number!

Say a color!

Do you like fruit salad?

Five!

Yellow!

Yes, I do.

79

1 Answer with a friend. Where does fruit come from?

2 Listen and read along. Label the pictures. 🎧75

blossom   fruit   plant   ~~seed~~

A Fruit Tree

Fruit is from *plants* or trees.

This is a *seed*. It's in the *ground*.

This is a plant. It needs *sunlight* and water to grow.

The plant is big now. It's a tree. Look! It has *blossoms*.

Now the tree has fruit. Look! Lots of oranges.

The oranges have seeds inside them. The seeds can grow again.

seed

3 Look and number.

1

4 Listen and match. 🎧76

This is a lemon tree.
It needs sunlight and water.

This is an orange tree.
Look! It has fruit.

5 Draw a tree and its fruit. Draw the weather.

6 Describe your drawings. Tell a friend. 💬

This is a _____. It needs _____.

Look! _____.

1 Trace the letter and complete the words.
Listen and repeat. 🎧 77

ch _o_ c ___ late   d ___ ct ___ r   fr ___ g   h ___ t   ___ ranges   s ___ cks

2 Listen and read. 🎧 78

Mom is a doctor. Look at her socks!
She likes hot cocoa and chocolates in a box.
Her friend is a frog. See his green legs?
He likes oranges, apples and eggs.

3 Listen again and repeat the chant.

A Cress-head Experiment

Materials

★ Two yogurt containers
★ Cotton balls
★ Water
★ Cress seeds
★ Pens

Monty's Value ...

★ **Read and stick.**

Eat fruit and vegetables every day.

 Stage 1: Plan your project.

1 Answer with a friend. What do plants need to grow?

2 Find a place in the sunlight and a place in the dark to grow your cress heads.

Stage 2: Develop your project.

1 Make two cress heads. Use clean yogurt containers.

2 Draw a happy face and a sad face on the containers.

3 Put cotton balls in the containers. Add water. Plant your seeds.

4 Put your happy cress head in the sun. Put the sad cress head in the dark.

5 Check your cress heads every day. Remember plants need water.

Stage 3: Share your project.

Present your cress heads to your classmates.

This plant is green.

This plant is yellow. Plants need sun.

Stage 4: Evaluate your project. 70

Save your *Project Record*.

1 **Listen, follow and color the number.** 79

2 **Look at Activity 1 and write sentences.**

1 ⭐6 <u>I like pears.</u> _____

2 ⭐2 _____

3 **Unscramble the questions and answer.**

like / Do / smoothies / ? / you

<u>Do you like smoothies?</u> _____

you / fruit / Do / like / salad?

_____ _____

like / you / Do / Jell-O / ?

_____ _____

1 Play *The Island Game.*

Madagascar

1 Look at the pictures. Can you name the plants and animals? 💬

2 Read and label the pictures.

baobab tree   fossa   ~~lemur~~

Hello! I'm Jenny. I'm seven. I'm from Madagascar. Madagascar is an *island* near Africa.
Look! What's this? It isn't a monkey. It's a *lemur.* What's this? It isn't a cat or a wolf. It's a *fossa*!
This is a tree. It's a *baobab* tree.
In Madagascar, you can find bananas, pineapples and mangoes!

lemur

3 Circle what you can find in your country.

baobab tree   bananas   fossa   lemur   mangoes   pineapples

4 Draw an animal from your country.

The History Project

1 **Look at the pictures and answer with a friend.** 💬

1 Where are Monty and Lola?   **2** What animals can you see?

2 **Listen and read along. Number the places Monty and Lola visit.** 🎧

☐ farm   1 desert   ☐ river   ☐ pyramid

1 Monty and Lola are in the classroom at school. This is the history teacher.

Now write about Egypt for homework.

Please put the books in the library.

OK! Come on, Monty!

2 Now Monty and Lola are in Ancient Egypt.

It's hot and sunny.

Hello! My name's Ra. This is the desert.

I'm wearing a dress!

3 Monty, Lola and Ra are in a pyramid.

These are Egyptian numbers.

One, two, three, four, five …

… six, seven, eight, nine, ten.

4 Monty, Lola and Ra see animals.

Look! Birds and a cat! *Egyptians like cats.*

I like cats, too.   *I don't like cats.*

5 Then Monty, Lola and Ra see a farm.

Here's a farmer. He has goats and ducks.

He has a bull, too.

It isn't a bull. It's a cow.

6 Monty, Lola and Ra are hungry.

Egyptians grow fruit. These are figs.

Do you like figs?

No, I don't, but I like grapes!

7 Now Monty, Lola and Ra are in a small boat.

This is the River Nile. It's very long.

There's the door to our library. Look!

8 One week later …

Here's your homework about Egypt. It's excellent!

Hurray!

Thank you!

Well done, Monty and Lola.

3 Act out the story.

87

Vocabulary

1 Answer with a friend.

1 Which toys do you like?
2 What's your favorite toy?

1
2
3
4
5
6
7
8
9
10

2 Listen, point and repeat. 🎧 81

3 Read, look and number.

ball ☐

doll ☐   guitar ☐   plane ☐

computer ☐   kite ☐   puppet ☐

dinosaur ☐   piano 1   robot ☐

88

4 Solve the crossword puzzle.

Across →

1 2 3 4 5

Down ↓

6 7 8 9 10

5 Circle the toys. Listen and act out. 🎵 82

I'm a magician. This is my hat.
Abracadabra! Look at that!
Abracadabra! One, two, three, four!
Here's a plane and a dinosaur!

Here's a robot, a puppet,
A guitar and a doll.
Here's a kite, a piano,
A computer and a ball.

I'm a magician. This is my hat…

6 Listen again and sing along.

7 Tell your friend. What toys do you have at home? 💬

I have a kite and a dinosaur.
The kite is my favorite.

I have a ball and a guitar.
The guitar is my favorite.

The Magic Hat

1 **Look at the pictures and answer with a friend.**

1 How many boys and girls are there? **2** What's in the magic hat?

2 **Listen and read along. Circle the toys the boys and girls want.**

 piano / ball   doll / kite   puppet / plane   robot / glue

1 This is Magic Mo. She's a magician. She has a magic hat. Here's Paul.

What do you want, Paul?

I want a ball, please.

2 Magic Mo makes magic.

Green frog! Black bat! I have a ball in my hat!

Oh! Thank you very much!

3 Here are the twins, Sol and Jane.

What do you want, Sol and Jane?

I want a plane, please.

I want a doll, please.

4 Magic Mo makes magic.

Green frog! Black bat! I have a doll and a plane in my hat!

Oh! Thank you very much!

5 Here's Lou.

What do you want, Lou?

GLUE

I want glue, please.

Glue?

Glue?

6 Lou opens his bag.

Yes! *I want glue*, please. My dinosaur is broken.

Aha! Put your dinosaur in my hat!

7 Magic Mo makes magic.

Green frog! Black bat! I have a dinosaur in my hat!

8 Look at Lou's dinosaur now!

Hurray! Thank you, Magic Mo!

That's magic!

3 Act out the story. 💬

91

1 **Listen and match.** 84

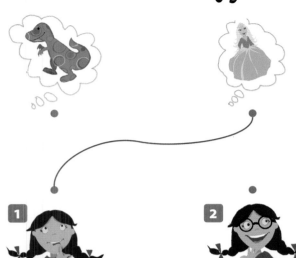

2 **Look at the pictures in Activity 1 and complete the sentences.**

1 I want a _____ doll _____ .   **3**  I want a _____ .

2 I want a _____ .   **4**  I want a _____ .

3 **Choose a card. Listen and play** *Toy-box Bingo!* 85

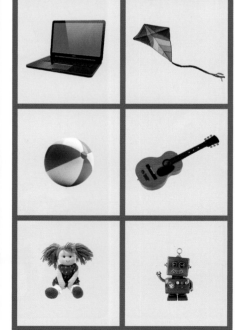
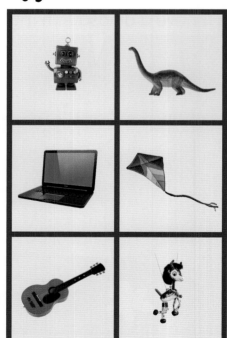

4 Write and match.

1 (piano) _I want a piano._

2 (kite) _____

3 (ball) _____

4 (computer) _____

5 Draw three toys in the magic hat. Write sentences.

Grammar

I want a doll.

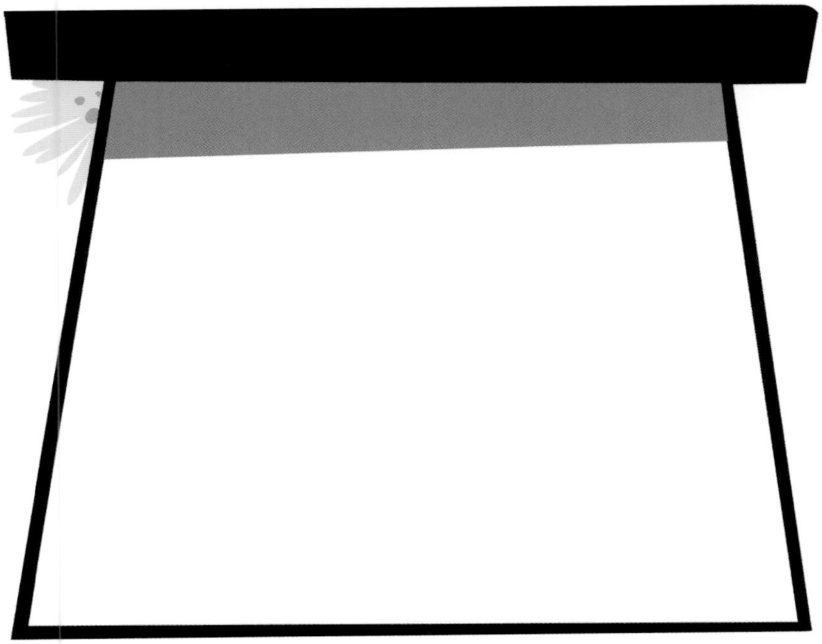

I want a _____

_____

_____

6 Tell a friend. Draw their toys.

I want a plane, please.

Lola's Tune

1 **Listen, point and repeat. Number the words.** 🎧 86

| 1 | 2 | 3 | 4 | 5 | 6 |

arms ☐ legs ☐ head ☐ tail ☐ hands ☐ 1 body ☐

2 **Look and complete. Listen and sing along.** 🎵 87

It has a body.
It has a **(1)** _____head_____.
It has one **(2)** _____.
It has one **(3)** _____.
It doesn't have hands.
It doesn't have feet.
It doesn't have a tail
And it doesn't have teeth.

Roar, roar, dinosaur!
Dinosaur, roar!
Roar, roar, dinosaur! Roar!

It has a **(4)** _____.
It has a head.
It has two arms.
It has two legs.
It has two **(5)** _____.
It has two feet.
Now it has a **(6)** _____
And very big teeth!

Roar, roar, dinosaur! …

3 **Look and circle.**

1 It (has)/ doesn't have a head.

2 It **has** / **doesn't have** hands.

3 It **has** / **doesn't have** a body.

4 It **has** / **doesn't have** a tail.

Grammar
It has legs.
It doesn't have arms.

4 Look and write *has* or *doesn't have*.

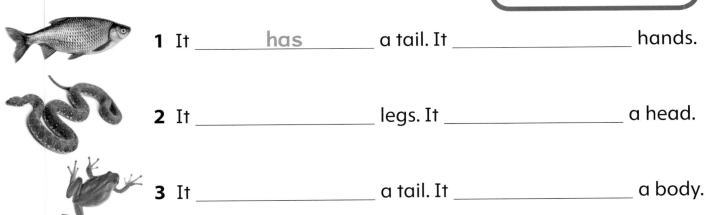

1 It _____has_____ a tail. It _____ hands.

2 It _____ legs. It _____ a head.

3 It _____ a tail. It _____ a body.

5 Complete the text with words from the box.

arms ~~arms~~   dinosaur   doll   hands

head   legs   robot   tail

Look at this animal. It doesn't have **(1)** _____arms_____.
It has four **(2)** _____ with big feet and toes.
It doesn't have **(3)** _____ or fingers. It has a small
(4) _____ with a small mouth. It has a long, spiky
(5) _____. What is it? It's a **(6)** _____.

6 Make *Dinosaur Cards*. Play with a friend. [W B] 115 💬

It has a big head and it has teeth.

This dinosaur!

95

1 **Describe your favorite toy to a friend.**

2 **Listen and read along. Can you find the lines of symmetry?**

Symmetry

Look at the robot. The two *sides* are the same. It is *symmetrical*. It has a *line of symmetry*.

Look at the plane. It is symmetrical. Look at the line of symmetry.

Look at the doll. The two sides are different. It is not symmetrical. It does not have a line of symmetry.

Look at this ball. It has two lines of symmetry!

3 **Mark (✔) the symmetrical toys. Draw the lines of symmetry.**

4 **Look and circle. Listen and check.**

This is a **kite** / **robot**. It's symmetrical. It has **one** / **two** line of symmetry.

This is a **plane** / **ball**. It's symmetrical. It has **one** / **two** lines of symmetry.

5 Draw a symmetrical toy. Draw the lines of symmetry.

6 Describe your drawing. Tell a friend.

This is a _____. It's _____.

It has _____.

1 Listen and write the missing sound. Listen again and repeat. 🎧 90

bird   hand   head   playground   red   san___

2 Listen and read. 🎧 91

I'm a dinosaur. This is my head.
My body is green. My legs are red.
This is my tail. This is my hand.
I'm in the playground in the sand.

3 Listen again and repeat the chant.

A Kite

Materials

* A long and short wooden stick
* Tape
* Plastic bags
* Scissors
* Yarn

 Read and stick.

Share your toys.

 ## Stage 1: Plan your project.

1 Answer with a friend. What shapes are kites? Why?
2 Draw a design for a kite in your notebook.

Stage 2: Develop your project.

1 Make a cross with two sticks. Tape them together.
2 Use your kite design. Draw the shape on a plastic bag. Cut it out.
3 Attach the plastic to the sticks.
4 Make a tail for your kite. Use tape to attach it.
5 Tie the yarn onto your kite.

Stage 3: Share your project.

1 Go outside. Fly your kite together!
2 Exchange kites with a friend. Share and learn!

Stage 4: Evaluate your project. 84

Save your *Project Record*.

This is our kite!
It's symmetrical.

1 **Listen, follow and color the number.**
Say a path for your friend. 🎧 92 💬

2 **Look at Activity 1 and write sentences.**

1 7 <u>I want a puppet.</u>

2 ⭐ 3 _____

3 **Look and describe the picture.**

(arms) <u>It doesn't have arms.</u>

(head) _____

(legs) _____

(tail) _____

8 Lola the Athlete

Vocabulary

1 **Answer with a friend.**

1 How many boys and girls are there? Describe them.

2 Who do you play with?

2 **Listen, point and repeat.** 93

3 **Read and trace.**

1 fly	**5** walk
2 climb	**6** hop
3 swing	**7** skate
4 swim	**8** run

9 jump

10 skip

4 Find ten action words.

1

2

3

4

5

q	a	z	s	w	i	n	g
w	f	l	y	a	s	x	e
d	c	r	v	l	h	o	p
t	j	g	s	k	a	t	e
r	u	n	b	s	w	i	m
y	m	h	n	k	u	j	m
i	p	c	l	i	m	b	k
o	l	p	m	p	n	b	v

6

7

8

9

10

5 Circle the action words. Listen and do the actions. 🎵 94

Now (hop) to the right! →
Walk one, two, three!
← Skate to the left
And jump with me!

Keep fit! Keep fit!
Shake it, shake it,
Shake it with me!

Keep fit! Keep fit!
Shake it, shake it,
Shake it with me!

Now swim to the right! →
Walk one, two, three!
← Skip to the left
And run with me!

Keep fit! Keep fit! …

Now fly to the right! →
Walk one, two, three!
← Swing to the left
And climb with me!

Keep fit! Keep fit! …

6 Listen again and sing along.

7 Play *Simon Says.*

Simon says jump!

Now climb!

Oops! Your turn!

The Gingerbread Man

1 Look at the pictures and answer with a friend.

1 Where is the *Gingerbread Man*?   2 What body parts does he have?

2 Listen and read along. Mark (✔) the actions in the story.

☐ climb ☐ fly ☐ hop ✔ jump ☐ run ☐ skate ☐ walk

1 One day, an old man and an old woman make gingerbread.

Now the gingerbread is ready!

Look at the Gingerbread Man!

2 But suddenly, the Gingerbread Man jumps off the table.

Hey!

I can jump! Yes, I can! *You can't catch me!* I'm the Gingerbread Man!

Oh no!

3 The Gingerbread Man, the old man and the old woman run to the river.

Stop, Gingerbread Man! Stop!

I can run! Yes, I can! *You can't catch me!* I'm the Gingerbread Man!

4 Then the Gingerbread Man, the old man and the old woman skate to the tree.

Stop, Gingerbread Man! Stop!

I can skate! Yes, I can! *You can't catch me!* I'm the Gingerbread Man!

5 Then the Gingerbread Man, the old man and the old woman climb the tree.

Stop, Gingerbread Man! Stop!

I can climb! Yes, I can! *You can't catch me!* I'm the Gingerbread Man!

6 Now the Gingerbread Man is in the tree. A bird is in the tree, too.

Oh no! *I can't fly!*

I can fly! Jump on my back!

7 But the bird wants to eat the Gingerbread Man.

I can fly! Yes, I can! And my favorite food is … Gingerbread Man!

Help!

Jump, Gingerbread Man! Jump!

8 The Gingerbread Man jumps.

I can jump! Yes, I can! *You CAN catch me!* I'm the Gingerbread Man!

Come on! Let's go home!

3 **Act out the story.** 💬

103

1 **Listen and number. Look and circle.** 96

I **can / can't** jump.　I **can / can't** run.　I **can** / **can't** skate.　I **can / can't** fly.

 2 **Listen and answer the questions.** 97

1 What's the boy's name? _____ Tom _____

2 How old is he? _____

3 What is his sister's name? _____

4 How old is she? _____

5 How many kites are there? _____

3 Listen and mark (✔) or (✘) for Tom and his sister. 🎧 98

Grammar

I can skate.

I can't fly.

4 Look and complete the sentences.

I _can swing_____. I _____.

I _____. _____.

5 Write what you can and can't do.

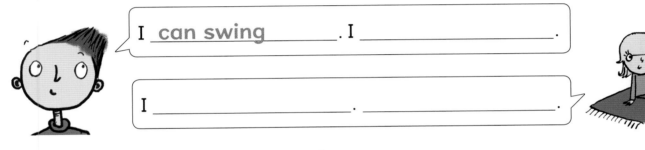

1 | 2 | 3 | 4

1 _I can skip._____ 3 _____

2 _____ 4 _____

6 Compare your answers with a friend. 💬

I can skip.
I can't climb.

I can climb.
I can't skate.

105

Monty's Tune

1 **Listen, point and repeat. Match.** 🎧 99

| kick a ball | drive a car | play a game |

| hit a ball | ride a bike | rollerblade |

2 **Circle the activities. Listen and play** *Activities Stand Up!* 🎵 100

Let's drive a car!
Let's ride a bike!
Come on, everyone! Let's play!

Let's drive a car!
Let's ride a bike!
Are you ready? It's a sunny day.

Let's hit a ball!
Let's kick a ball!
Come on, everyone! Let's play!

Let's hit a ball!
Let's kick a ball!
Are you ready? It's a sunny day.

Let's play a game!
Let's rollerblade!
Come on, everyone! Let's play!

Let's play a game!
Let's rollerblade!
Are you ready? It's a sunny day.
Are you ready? It's a sunny day.

3 **Listen again and sing along.**

4 **Look and complete the sentences.**

1 Let's ride ___a bike___.

2 Let's drive _____.

3 Let's _____.

4 Let's play _____.

5 Let's hit _____.

6 Let's kick _____.

5 Unscramble the sentences. Number the pictures.

1 ride / Let's / bike / a /!

  Let's ride a bike!

2 a / Let's / ! / drive / car

  _____

3 kick / ball / a / Let's!

  _____

4 play / a / game / Let's / !

  _____

5 hit / Let's / ball/ ! / a

  _____

> **Grammar**
>
> Let's play a game!

6 Look and write sentences. What can you do with these objects?

1 Let's rollerblade.

2 _____

3 _____

4 _____

7 Make the game. Play with a friend. [WB] 113

Let's play a game.

Let's rollerblade.

1 Answer with a friend. What activities do you do in P.E.?

2 Listen and read along. Write the numbers. 🎧 101

| ~~6~~ | 10 | 15 |

Distances

We measure distances in Physical Education (P.E.) to show what we can do. We can measure distances in *meters* (m) and *centimeters* (cm).

Look! Dan can kick a ball __6__ meters.

Sam can swim ___ meters.

Ben can jump one meter and ___ centimeters.

1 2 3 4

What's your personal best?

3 Guess and write how far you can hop. Draw a blue line.

1 square = 1 meter

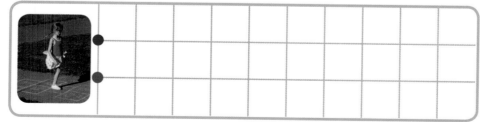

My guess: _____ m

My distance: _____ m

4 Do the activity with a friend. Measure and write the distance. Draw a red line.

5 Listen and circle. 🎧 102

I can **jump** / **throw** a ball **two** / **three** meters.

I can **kick** / **hit** a ball **seven** / **nine** meters.

⑥ **Guess and write the distances. Do the sports. Write the distances.**

Activity	My Guess	My Distance
 jump		
throw a ball		
kick a ball		

⑦ **Describe your results. Tell a friend.**

I can _____.

① **Trace the letters and complete the words.
Listen and repeat.** 🎧 103

| ar |

c <u>a r</u>   d___k   f___m   g___den   guit___   p___k

② **Listen and read.** 🎧 104

Charlie the cow can't play the guitar.
He doesn't have arms, but he can drive a car.
He can drive in the garden. He can drive in the park.
He can drive at the farm. He can drive in the dark.

③ **Listen again and repeat the chant.**

Activities Challenge

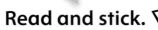

Materials

* ★ Sports equipment (soccer ball, tennis ball, jump rope, bat, cones)
* ★ A watch
* ★ A meter stick
* ★ Paper
* ★ Pen

★ **Read and stick.**

Be a good team player!

 Stage 1: Plan your project.

1 Make a list of different activities you practice in your P.E. class.

2 Design a challenge to measure the distance or time for four activities.

3 Draw a chart in your notebook.

Stage 2: Develop your project.

1 Take your equipment to the playground.

2 Take turns trying each activity challenge. Time your friends. Measure the distances.

3 Write down your friends' results in your chart.

Activities Challenge	My Friends' Results
Kick a ball 10 meters	Tom: 8 meters Clare: 10 meters Luis: 11 meters
Jump 1 meter	Tom: 1 meter 10 centimeters Clare: 90 centimeters Luis: 1 meter 5 centimeters
Run 100 meters 30 seconds	Tom: 32 seconds Clare: 28 seconds Luis: 30 seconds
Throw a ball 5 meters	Tom: 6 meters Clare: 5 meters Luis: 5 meters

Stage 3: Share your project.

Present your results to your classmates.

Tom can kick a ball eight meters.

Stage 4: Evaluate your project. **WB** 94

Save your *Activities Challenge Chart*.

1 **Listen, follow and color the number.**
 Say a path for your friend. 🎧 105 💬

2 **Look at Activity 1 and write sentences.**

1 ⭐1 <u>I can swing.</u>   2 ⭐4 _____

_____   _____

_____   _____

3 **Circle three activities. Play *Let's Go* with a friend.** 💬

Let's play a game.

No, thanks. Let's drive a car.

Yes! Let's drive a car.

1 Play *Maze Run*!

I want …

It has …

I can …

Let's …

I can't …

I can't …

It has …

It doesn't have …

I want …

It doesn't have …

I can …

Let's …

It has …

I can …

It has …

I can't …

I want …

It doesn't have …

I can't …

Let's …

Let's …

I can …

It doesn't have …

I want …

United States of America

1 Look at the pictures and answer with a friend. 💬

1 Can you name the sports? **2** Which sports can you do?

2 Read and complete. | jump   skate   hit a ball |

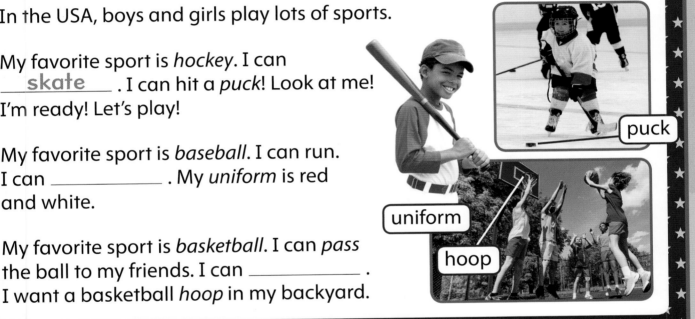

In the USA, boys and girls play lots of sports.

My favorite sport is *hockey*. I can ___skate___ . I can hit a *puck*! Look at me! I'm ready! Let's play!

My favorite sport is *baseball*. I can run. I can _____ . My *uniform* is red and white.

My favorite sport is *basketball*. I can *pass* the ball to my friends. I can _____ . I want a basketball *hoop* in my backyard.

puck

uniform

hoop

3 Draw and label the sports in the USA. Draw and label popular sports in your country.

Popular Sports

The USA   My Country

9 Monty the Diver

1 Answer with a friend.

1 What's the weather like?

2 What can you do at the beach?

2 Listen, point and repeat. 🎧 106

3 Read and match.

1 sun	**2** sky	**3** tree	**4** beach	**5** sand
6 sea	**7** turtle	**8** fish	**9** shell	**10** rock

4 Circle ten words. Label the pictures.

beachfishrocksandseashellskysuntreeturtle

| 1 _____ | 2 _____ | 3 _____ | 4 _____ | 5 _beach_ |

| 6 _____ | 7 _____ | 8 _____ | 9 _____ | 10 _____ |

5 Circle what you can see at the beach. Listen and sing along. 107

I can see the (sky) I can see the sun.
I can see a big tree, too.
I can see the beach. I can see the sand.
I can see the sea. It's blue.

Splish! Splash! Under the sea.
Swim, swim! Swim with me.
Splish! Splash! Under the sea.
Swim, swim! Swim with me.

I can see a shell. I can see a fish.
I can see a turtle, too.
I can see a rock. I can see a ship.
I can see the sea. It's blue.

Splish! Splash! Under the sea.
Swim, swim! Swim with me.
Splish! Splash! Under the sea.
Swim, swim! Swim with me.

6 Play *I Can See …* with a friend.

I can see something that starts with *B*!

Yes! Your turn!

Beach!

Where's the Turtle?

1 **Look at the pictures and answer with a friend.** 💬

   1 Where is the mermaid?   **2** How many fish can you find?

2 **Listen and read along. Number the speech bubbles in order.** 🎧 108

| Hurray! ☐ | It's a rock. ☐ | Let's look! 1 | It's a shell! ☐ | It's my friend! ☐ |

1 One day a mermaid sees a crab. The crab is sad.

> I can't find my friend. He's a turtle.

> Don't worry! Let's look!

2 The mermaid and the crab swim in the sea. Then the crab sees something.

> Is it a turtle?

> No, it isn't. It's a shell.

3 So the mermaid and the crab swim in the sea. Then the crab sees something.

> Is it a turtle?

> No, it isn't. It's a rock.

4 So the mermaid and the crab swim in the sea. Then the crab sees something.

> Is it a turtle?

> No, it isn't. It's a big fish. Eek!

5 The mermaid and the crab can't find the turtle. But suddenly …

What's that noise?

Knock Knock

I don't know.

6 The mermaid and the crab find a chest.

What's in the chest?

Knock Knock

Is it a turtle?

7 The mermaid opens the chest.

Yes, it is!

Phew! Thank you.

It's my friend!

8 The mermaid, the crab and the turtle are very happy.

Here's the turtle …

Hurray!

Yippee!

… and look at the treasure!

3 Act out the story. 💬

1 **Listen and number. Look and trace.** 🎧 109

Is it a turtle?
Yes, it is.
No, it isn't.

Is it a turtle?
Yes, it is.
No, it isn't.

Is it a turtle?
Yes, it is.
No, it isn't.

Is it a turtle?
Yes, it is.
No, it isn't.

2 **Connect the dots. Write the short answers.**

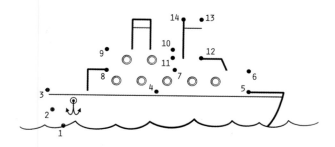

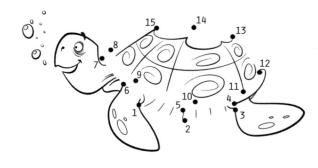

1 Is it a rock?   <u>No, it isn't.</u>

2 Is it sand?   _____

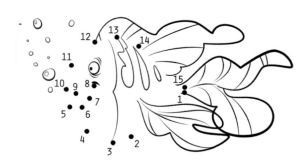

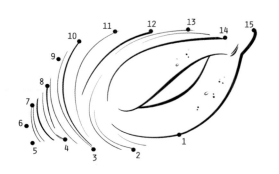

3 Is it a fish?   _____

4 Is it a shell?   _____

3 Unscramble the questions. Answer with a friend.

1  the / Is / it / ? / sun   *Is it the sun?*

2 it / a / ? / tree / Is   _____

3  ? / sea / the / Is / it   _____

4 it / ? / beach / a / Is   _____

4 Look and answer the questions.

1

Is it a turtle?   *Yes, it is.*

2

Is it a rock?   _____

3

Is it the sky?   _____

4

Is it a shell?   _____

5 Play *Draw and Guess* with a friend.

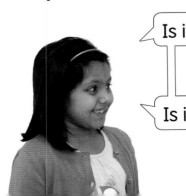

Is it a shell?

No, it isn't.

Is it a fish?

Yes, it is! Your turn!

Lola's Tune

1 Listen, point and repeat. Trace. 🎧 110

 dolphins    crabs

 penguins   seals

seagulls   snails

2 Listen and point to the animals. Listen again and sing along. 🎵 111

They're dolphins. They're dolphins.
They're dolphins in the sea.
They're penguins. They're penguins.
One, two and three.

Oh, yeah!

They're seals. They're seals.
They're seals on the shore.
They're crabs. They're crabs.
One, two, three and four.

Oh, yeah!

They're seagulls. They're seagulls.
They're seagulls in the sky.
They're snails. They're snails.
One, two, three, four and five.

Oh, yeah!

3 Look and complete the sentences.

1 They're ___seagulls___ .   3 They're _____ .   5 They're _____ .

2 They're _____ .   4 They're _____ .   6 They're _____ .

4 Look and answer the questions.

1 How many animals are in the picture? _Fourteen_____.
2 They can fly. What are they? They're _____.
3 Which animals are on the rock? The _____.
4 How many crabs are in the picture? _____.
5 They're in the sea. What are they? They're _____.

5 Read the clues and write sentences.

Sea Animals Quiz!

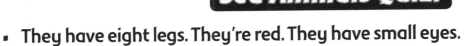

- They have eight legs. They're red. They have small eyes. _They're crabs._
- They don't have legs. They have shells. They can't swim. _____
- They're black and white. They can swim. _____
- They're big and gray. They can swim. _____

6 Make the game. Play with a friend.

They're dolphins.

They're dolphins. SNAP!

121

1 Answer with a friend. What can instruments sound like?

2 Listen and read along. Point to the pictures. 112

Water Music

Music can be *fast*. Music can be *slow*. Music can be *quiet*. Music can be *loud*. Listen to the water music.

This is music about the *sea*. It's fast and loud. This is music about *rain*. It's quiet and slow.

This is music about a *stream*. It's fast and quiet.

Can music make pictures in your head? Listen again and draw a picture.

3 Look and imagine the music. Circle the best words.

(quiet)   fast

loud   slow

quiet   fast

loud   slow

quiet   fast

loud   slow

4 Look and complete the words. Listen and check. 113

This is r _a_ _i_ n. The music is
qu ___ ___ ___. It's s ___ ___ w.

This is the s ___ ___. The music is
l ___ ___ d. It's f ___ ___ t.

5 Draw a picture with water. Imagine the music.

6 Describe your drawing. Describe the music. Tell a friend. 💬

This is _____.

The music is _____.

1 Trace the letter and complete the words.
Listen and repeat. 🎧 114

s

_s_ and   ___eagulls   ___eals   ___ix   ___even   ___un

2 Listen and read. 🎧 115

Seven snails in the sun.
Six seals in the sea.
Seven sisters on the sand.
Six seagulls in the tree.

3 Listen again and repeat the chant.

My Beach Collage

Lola's Value...

Materials

★ Paper
★ Paints
★ Recycled paper and plastic bags
★ Recycled candy wrappers
★ Recycled bottle caps
★ Glue stick

 Read and stick.

Keep the beach clean!

Stage 1: Plan your project.

1 Draw a picture of the beach, the sea and the sky. Paint your picture.

2 Write a list of animals to include in your collage.

3 Answer with a friend. How can you keep the beach clean?

Stage 2: Develop your project.

1 Write a title on your picture.

2 Use recycled trash to illustrate the animals in your collage. For example, is it gray? Can it be a dolphin?

3 Label the animals in your collage.

Stage 3: Share your project.

Present your collage to your classmates.

This is my collage! They're fish. Please keep the beach clean!

Stage 4: Evaluate your project. 106

Save your *Beach Collage*.

1 **Listen, follow and color the number.**
   Say a path for your friend. 🎧 116 💬

2 **Look at Activity 1 and write the questions and answers.**

1 ⭐8 Is it the sun? _____ No, it isn't. _____

   _____ _____

   _____ _____

3 **Look and write sentences. What are they?**

They're dolphins. _____ _____

_____ _____

1 Look at the pictures and answer with a friend.

1 What sport do Monty and Lola play?   2 What colors are their uniforms?

2 Listen and read along. Mark (✔) or (✘) what Monty and Lola can do. 🎧 117

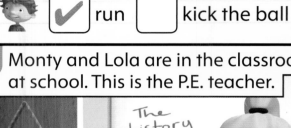 ✔ run ☐ kick the ball   ☐ kick the ball ☐ jump

1 Monty and Lola are in the classroom at school. This is the P.E. teacher.

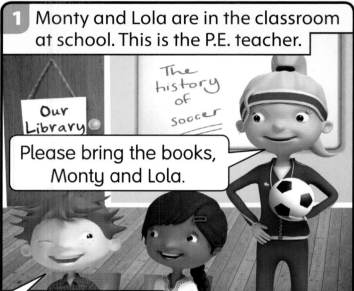

Please bring the books, Monty and Lola.

OK! Come on, Lola!

2 Now Monty and Lola are in a big soccer stadium.

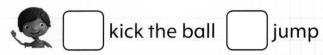

Wow! *It's the World Cup!* We're soccer players! He's the referee. *He has a whistle.*

Fantastic! *I can play soccer.*

3 Monty and Lola are on the red team.

Oh no! Look at the score!

Come on, Lola! *Let's play!*

4 Monty has the ball, but this player is very big. He has long legs.

I'm small …

… but I'm fast!

5 Look at Monty!

I can run and I can kick the ball!

Yes!

Goal!

6 Now the score is 2–2. Lola has the ball.

Oh no! I can't kick the ball!

Come on, Lola!

7 Lola can't kick the ball, but she can jump.

With your head, Lola!

Oh no!

Goal!

8 The red team is the winner! Monty and Lola have the prize.

Hurray!

Well done, Monty and Lola!

Aw! I want the prize!

3 Act out the story.

127

Syllabus

	Vocabulary	Structures	Phonics	Cross-Curricular Themes	Cultural Values
S	Classroom Objects Numbers 1–20	Hello! I'm (Monty / six).			
1	Colors School Objects	It's (red). It's my / your (pencil).	artist handprint	Art: Abstract Art	Keeping the classroom organized
2	Parts of the Face and Body Items to Keep us Clean	I have (a nose / ears). This is his / her (soap).	toothbrush mouth	Science: Teeth	Taking care of your teeth
3	Family Physical Descriptions	This is my (aunt). These are my (cousins). He has (blue) eyes. She has (long) hair.	brother sister	Science: Twins	Spending time with your family
4	Clothes Weather	I'm wearing (a hat / socks). It's (snowing).	sunny jungle	Geography: Climates	Working together
5	Farm Animals Baby Animals	It isn't (a swan). It's (a frog). Where's my (chick)? It's here.	chick chicken	Music: Peter and the Wolf	Listening to others
6	Fruit Food Made from Fruit	a banana / an orange I like (pineapples). I don't like (frogs). Do you like (smoothies)? Yes, I do. / No, I don't.	oranges doctor	Science: A Fruit Tree	Eating fruit and vegetables every day
7	Toys Parts of the Body	I want (a doll). It has (a body). It doesn't have (legs).	red head	Maths: Symmetry	Sharing your toys
8	Actions Outdoor Activities	I can (skate). I can't (fly). Let's (drive a car)!	farm guitar	P.E.: Distances	Being a good team player
9	Seaside Objects Sea Animals	Is it (a turtle)? Yes, it is. / No, it isn't. a / the turtle They're (dolphins).	seagulls sun	Music: Water Music	Keeping the beach clean